Natalia, With Love

Youssef Khalim

ISBN: 978-0-9787810-6-4
ISBN-13: 978-0978781064

DEDICATION

To: Lori (The real or ideal soul mate: inspiration)

Tonya Tracy Khalim and

Runako Soyini Khalim, (my most beloved daughters)

Mother and Grandmother and Great-grandmother, (my most beloved maternal biological ancestors, and spiritual antecedents)

M. A. Garvey (one of my 7 M's: my role models)

Youssef Khalim II; III (my most beloved sons)

Father and Grandfather and Great-grandfather, (my most beloved paternal biological ancestors, and spiritual antecedents)

To: The Forerunners and Reincarnation sources (beloved biological ancestors and spiritual antecedents), and

The Almighty (our Spiritual Father), from whence we come.

CONTENTS

ACKNOWLEDGMENTS

To: The Forerunners and Reincarnation sources (beloved biological ancestors and spiritual antecedents), and

The Almighty (our Spiritual Father), from whence we come.

1 INTRODUCTION

I was born July 29, 1977, in a small village, near Samara, Russia. And I love to be photographed. I am logical, rational, and intelligent, or so I've been told. My friends say it is great fun to be around me because I sometimes joke around, and have a good sense of humor.

I became interested in modeling in Samara, and I intend to pursue it as a major goal. I am 5'8" tall, and I weigh 125 pounds. I have grey eyes. Currently, I work as an Ecologist, in Samara. My dream, later, is to marry and have children.

September 9, 2004,
Natalia

Natalia, With Love is the fourth in a series of eight books by Youssef Khalim, begun in 2002. Four were inspired by ladies encountered over- seas. Natalia is one of the four overseas encounters.

I met Natalia in the summer of 2004, over the Internet. I saw her photo on New-Dating.Com, and emailed her. Later, I was struck by her extraordinary beauty and lovely personality. I wrote down my feelings, thoughts, and moods as fast as I could. Natalia is the motivation and inspiration for this book.

Sometimes it seemed that the book was writing itself, and I was only a channel, trying to keep up. First, came *I Fell In-Love With You Instantly*. Then, the other selections followed rapidly, and the book was complete in about two weeks, working part time. This is a must-read.

Natalia has the most gorgeous, and sexy body, and attractive and charismatic personality, and I have attempted to capture and reflect her awesome presence and personality in *Natalia, With Love*. Enjoy.

September 9, 2004,
Youssef Khalim

2 I FELL IN-LOVE WITH YOU INSTANTLY

Your awesome beauty
Shocked and stunned
My body - and mind,

And I fell in-love
With you instantly,
Just after I recovered.

3 IN THIS WILDERNESS

I love working with you,
Being your photographer, and assistant.

I love to scan you, pan you,
View you, up close.
Handle you, professionally,
Help you with your bra and bikini,
Put lotion and repellent on you.

Put away my camera,
Manhandle you,
Kiss you,
Hold you,
And love you,
Madly,
Wildly,
In this wilderness,

Before we resume our work.

4 I ADMIT IT – I NEED YOU

I like to think, I'm strong,
Independent,
Self-sufficient,
Self-sustaining,
And whole.

But, I admit,
I need you,
To love.

Your softness and your energy
Focus,
Strengthen,
Give direction,

Inspire me,
Motivate,
And energize me,
Give me life,
With meaning.

I need to hold you,
Caress you,
Soak myself, and
Love you, more and more,
(My precious gift),
Sent down to earth,
To truly make me whole.

5 I GOT HOOKED ON YOU

I got addicted to your love
Yes, I got hooked on you.

I got used to you, in my arms,
I got so high on you.

I got strung-out,
You were my drug of choice.

But, I recovered; I woke up,
And I got my voice back.

I'm getting better day by day,
I finally found a way.

I don't love you, more each day.
I love you day by day.

No, I don't love you, more each day.
I love you day by day.

I'm taking responsibility,
And acting like a man,

I kicked you as a habit,
And love you when I can.

6 YOU ARE THE EVIDENCE

God comes down to earth,
Takes on Her human form,
Makes music, songs,
And things to play them on,

And take us flying across the sky,
To be together forever,

And show just how clever and smart
You - are
Becoming.

7 SOMETIMES

Sometimes,

During the day, I miss you, and want you.

This is such a time.

I LOVE YOU.

Love,
Me.

8 ALL I EVER WANT

You are

All

I would ever want

In a woman.

9 MEN WHO CAME DOWN FROM HEAVEN

You can always tell
The men who
Came down from heaven:

They love, respect, and adore:
Women and children,
(Especially their own),
And God,
And people.

They love beauty, truth, and justice,
Because they remind them
Of where they came from,

And they come down to earth
To be with you.

10 I LOVE TO TAKE A SHOWER WITH YOU

I come in,
After you're wet,
And touch you,
Hold you,
Kiss your warm, sweet mouth,
Caress, explore your heavenly body,
And tease you with some love.

Then, find a cozy place,
To take our time,
And love you
Until times gives up, and stops!

Fulfill your current and future needs for fantasy!
Take you places "in-the making"

Love you, divinely,
Over and over.

Then, gently bring you back to earth,
Refreshed, and sparkling,

Just like when we left the shower.

11 YOU ASK: WHO, OR WHAT IS GOD?

God is that force that brings you into existence,
In the physical world,
And He takes you out.

God creates the weather, the seasons,
worlds, the reasons.

Even hurricanes and tornados
Are spin-offs of Our Cosmic Mind,
And sometimes difficult to understand.

But everything moves and has its being
In God.
(And God is life and love)

And hurricanes and tornadoes
Are somewhat like chemotherapy,
Destroying illusions about our physical world,
Bodies, reality, and egos
By our own collective and personal souls,
To show: the Universe is ruled by love,
Togetherness, acceptance, cooperation.
We have our personal niche in God.
We are immortal, souls,
Rooted in the heart of God,
Felt as, and feeling, love.
And not just physical shells.

And the existence of selfishness, greed, and injustice,
Must be uprooted,
To make way for
Our New World of love.

Now, to answer you directly:
You are rooted in my heart,
Like we have root in God.

12 A BAD GIRL WILL DO

When you left,
You left a hole in my soul.

You left me desperate, in-love
Without a good girl to love.

I looked around in desperation,
Trying to find some satisfaction,
Trying to find a good girl
For your space.

Someone to take your place,
In my life.

I looked uptown, downtown,
All around the Internet,
Trying to get,
A good girl, just like you.

Someone to give my heart to,
Someone to be a part of me.

I want a girl who is true
A girl just like you.

I'm looking everywhere,
For a girl who will care.

I want a girl just like you
To give my love to.

And if I can't find another you,
A bad girl will do,

If she fills up the hole in my soul.

13 IT WAS GREAT SEEING YOU TODAY

You get more beautiful, day, by day.

And I just love to see you:
Your smile,
Your lovely eyes, and sexy mouth,
I love your nose, and gorgeous face.

I love to see you walk.
That really turns me on!

I want to hold you, love your
Sexy, curvy hips, completely - but, It's not possible now.

So, I'll love your gorgeous legs.
Your legs are fantastic.

You make me want my own
Fantastic "Baby Doll,"
To give me heaven every day
Blow me away,
And give me heaven now!

OK. I love your warm, sweet conversation too,
I love to hear you, hear your voice.
I love you as my very first choice.

I'll love you now, forever,
Rejoice in you, in the hereafter,
And love you completely,
On this or any day.

14 OUR PATTERN IS SET FOREVER

I love you because of patterns in the stars.

Consider how lovely snowflakes form.
The internal/external factors:

The hydrogen, oxygen, location, position
Atmosphere, temperature, and sun/moon, wind influence.

And consider leaves and trees.

We form, are formed in patterns, cycles
By internal/external factors.

Consider, I was born on April 13, 1743, the 3rd of six children,
And on June, 6, 1944, the 3rd of six children,
Became the 3rd president of the USA.
Was the 3rd patriarch of 42,
Listed in the Book of Matthew,
My name means twin, over and over,
Lifetime after lifetime: Gemini, Jacob, Thomas, Jimmy, James.

I was a soldier, in 1637, when the Christians
Got expelled from Japan,
Saw many lifetimes, in many lands,
And know that Muhammad is Moses, reincarnated,
As was his pattern, and say his words, and is my vision.

And this is how this relates to you:
Formed When the patterns in the stars
Were fantastically beautiful, sexy,
Lovely, exotic, and intelligent.

And I was born this time,
To find you,
And love you, forever,
Completely,

Because our pattern is set:
I will always find you, and love you,
Set by patterns in the stars.

15 I LOVE IT WHEN YOU GIVE YOURSELF TO ME

I love it, when you say,
"I love you."

I love it when
You give yourself to me.

I love to feel your warm breath
On my neck,

I love to hold you in my arms,
And feel your body,
Hot, against mine.

I love to touch you, kiss you, love you,
Give you joy, and bliss, and heaven,
Show how much I love you,

Lose our selves,
In-love,
And love it!

Whenever, wherever, however,
You give yourself to me.

16 I LISTENED TO SOME MUSIC

I heard Soulful Strut, by Young-Holt Unlimited,
About a month ago, and it blew me away.
It got me listening, to music.

I got the lyrics, called, "Am I The Same Girl?"
My world started spinning to music.

I got the CD's of Kim Waters, and others,
Got "I'm Ready," by Tevin Campbell,
And Quincy Jones, Baby Face, and team.

I listened to Mariah Carey's "Mariah,"
R. Kelley's "Step, In The Name of Love,"
Luther Vandross and Whitney.
And, now I make this witness:
Music is magic,
Amazing, calming, and fantastic.
It's special, satisfying; goes well with loving you.

Yes, music is magic, calming, and fantastic.

Now, I knew that,
And you know that,
So please take time to listen.

17 TO MAKE A PLACE FOR YOU

We sat quietly, thinking,
Sometimes, third eye, looking,
Waiting at the threshold, to grab insight, or truth.

We were Shamen, spiritual leaders, Prophet-Kings/Philosopher-Priests.

Saw awesome visions, things so nearly real:
Where matter changes, in the Spirit World.

Our work required integrity, rigorous honesty,
Objectivity and subjectivity.

My most important findings were:

Moses reincarnated as Prophet Muhammad,
Seen in vision, on 5/2/2000,

I am the reincarnation of Thomas Jefferson,
Seen in vision on 8/4/1999,

My first son died at two months old,
Came back as daughter #2, four years later,
(She was once my twin).

I saw spacecraft, in visions/dreams, in-flight,
That seem more real than life,

The USA is part of the eighth and last World Empire,
As predicted by Daniel, and John, The Revelator.

As Jefferson, I doubled the size of the USA,
Adding lands from the Mississippi to the Rockies,
Gave it ideals, and more, forevermore:

The Bill Of Rights, lands west of Virginia,
Manifest Destiny, to become the last empire.

We bridged the way for the Africans,
Came back to be their advocate.

For example, the 12 Electoral Votes for my reign
Came from the Africans, making them rightful heirs
To this, and Kingdoms To Come.

And the number 12, here, being the appropriate "Jacob" symbol,
Pattern, and key, as a good shaman can readily see.

We traveled to the worlds of exotic beauty, love,
And old, yet new experiences:

Which is how I came to meet you:

I was shocked and stunned
By your sexy, awesome beauty,

Which knocked a hole, right in my soul,
To make a place for you.

18 CHRISTIANITY AND ISLAM SHOW BELIEF IN REINCARNATION (ALSO, OUR UNITY; THE UNITY OF MAN)

I want to say this short and sweet,
In a few short words,

From The Muslim and Christian Holy Books,
How reincarnation works,

But, it' not easy, in a few short words,
So, Let us try this way.

Maybe, someday, we'll have,
A sweeter, shorter list,

Then, we'll resist temptation,

And all *this* talk about Unity,
And *talk* about how life works:

39:42 says:
It is Allâh Who takes away the souls at the time of their death, and those that die not during their sleep. He keeps those souls for which He has ordained death and sends the rest for a term appointed. Verily, in this are signs for a people who think deeply.

Then, 6:60 says:
It is He, Who takes your souls by night (when you are asleep), and has knowledge of all that you have done by day, then he raises (wakes) you up again that a term appointed (your life period) be fulfilled, then in the end unto Him will be your return. Then He will inform you what you used to do.

And 6:61 says:
He is the Irresistible, Supreme over His subjects, and **He sends guardians (angels guarding and writing all of one's good and bad deeds) over you, until when death approaches one of you, Our Messengers (angel of death and his assistants) take his soul, and they never neglect their duty.**

6:62 says:
Then they are returned to Allâh, their Maulâ (God), the Just Lord (to reward them). **Surely, His is the judgment and He is the Swiftest in taking account.**

And 2:28 says:

How can you disbelieve in Allâh? Seeing that you were dead and He gave you life. Then He will give you death, then again will bring you to life and then unto Him you will return.

3:145 says:

And no person can ever die except by Allâh's Leave and at an appointed term. **And whoever desires a reward in (this) world, We shall give him of it; and whoever desires a reward in the Hereafter, We shall give him thereof. And We shall reward the grateful.**

And 3:168 says:

Think not of those who are killed in the Way of Allâh as dead. Nay, they are alive, with their Lord, **and they have provision.**

16:70 says:

And Allâh has created you and then He will cause you to die, and of you there are some who are sent back to senility, so that they know nothing after having known (much). **Truly! Allâh is All- Knowing, All-Powerful.**

And 22:6 says:

That is because Allâh, He is the Truth, and it is He Who gives life to the dead, and it is He Who is Able to do all things.

22:7 says:

And surely, the Hour is coming, there is no doubt about it, and certainly, Allâh will resurrect those who are in the graves.

And 6:94 says:

And truly you have come unto Us alone **(without wealth, companions or anything else)** as We created you *the first time.* **You have left behind you all that which We had bestowed on you.** ***We see not with you your intercessors whom you claimed to be partners with Allâh.*** **Now all relations between you and them have been cut off, and all that you used to claim has vanished from you.**

6:95 says:
Verily! It is Allâh Who causes the seed–grain and the fruit–stone (like date–stone, etc.) to split and sprout. **He brings forth the living from the dead, and it is He Who brings forth the dead from the living.** Such is Allâh, then how are you deluded away from the truth?

And 6:59 says:
And with Him are the keys of the Ghaib (all that is hidden), none knows them but He. And He knows whatever there is in (or on) the earth and in the sea; not a leaf falls, but *he knows it.* **There is not a grain in the darkness of the earth nor anything fresh or dry,** but is written in a *Clear Record.*

Now, Matthew 9 says:
23) And when Jesus came into the ruler's house, and saw the minstrels and the people making a noise,

24) He said unto them, Give place: for the maid is not dead, but sleepeth. **And they laughed him to scorn.**

25) But when the people were put forth, **he went in, and took her by the hand, and the maid arose.**

And Matthew 11 says:
2) Now when John had heard in the prison the works of Christ, he sent two of his disciples,

3) And said unto him, Art thou he that should come, or do we look for another?

13) For **all the prophets and the law prophesied until John.**

14) And if ye will receive it, **this is Elijah, which was for to come.**

Matthew 14 says:
2) And said unto his servants, This is John the Baptist; he is
risen from the dead; and therefore mighty works do shew forth themselves in him.

And Matthew 16 says:
13) When Jesus came into the coasts of Caesarea Philippi, he asked his disciples, saying, Whom do men say that I the Son of man am?

And they said, **Some say that thou art John the Baptist: some, Elias; and others, Jeremias, or one of the prophets.**

14) He saith unto them, But whom say ye that I am?

15) And Simon Peter answered and said, **Thou art the Christ, the Son of the living God.**

28) **Verily I say unto you, There be some standing here, which shall not taste of death, till they see the Son of man coming in his kingdom.**

Chapter 17:
1) And after six days Jesus taketh Peter, James, and John his brother, and bringeth them up into an high mountain apart,

2) And **was transfigured before them: and his face did shine as the sun, and his raiment was white as the light.**

3) And, behold, t**here appeared unto them Moses and Elias talking with him.**

4) Then answered Peter, and said unto Jesus, Lord, it is good for us to be here: if thou wilt, **let us make here three tabernacles; one for thee, and one for Moses, and one for Elias.**

5) While he yet spake, behold, a bright cloud overshadowed them: and behold a voice out of the cloud, which said, **This is my be- loved Son, in whom I am well pleased; hear ye him.**

9) And as they came down from the mountain, Jesus charged them, saying, Tell the ***vision*** to no man, until **the Son of man be risen again from the dead.**

10) And his disciples asked him, saying, **Why then say the scribes that Elias must first come?**

11) And **Jesus answered and said unto them, Elias truly shall first come, and restore all things,**

12) But I say unto you, **That Elias is come already, and they knew him not, but have done unto him whatsoever they listed.** Likewise shall also the Son of man suffer of them.

Then the disciples understood that he spake unto them of John the Baptist.

Now Matthew 17, 22, and 23; Mark 9, and 12; Luke 8 and 9, John 1, 4, and 5 give confirming, and similar messages.

John 5 says:
26) For as the Father hath life in himself; so hath he given to the Son to have life in himself;

28) Marvel not at this: for the hour is coming, in the which **all that are in the graves shall hear his voice,**

29) ***And shall come forth; they that have done good, unto the resurrection of life; and they that have done evil, unto the resurrection of damnation.***

Now, John 6, 10,11, and 17 put forth a similar message. And Acts 2 says:
42) And they continued steadfastly in the apostles' doctrine and fellowship, and in breaking of bread, and in prayers.

43) And fear came upon every soul: and many wonders and signs were done by the apostles.

44) And **all that believed were together, and had all things common;**

45) And sold their possessions and goods, **and parted them to all men, as every man had need.**

46) And they, continuing daily with one accord in the temple, and breaking bread from house to house, did eat their meat with gladness and singleness of heart,

47) Praising God, and having favour with all the people. And the Lord added to the church daily such as should be saved.

Acts 4 says:
30) By stretching forth thine hand to heal; and that signs and wonders may be done by the name of thy holy child Jesus.

31) And when they had prayed, the place was shaken where they

Then the disciples understood that he spake unto them of John the Baptist.

Now Matthew 17, 22, and 23; Mark 9, and 12; Luke 8 and 9, John 1, 4, and 5 give confirming, and similar messages.

John 5 says:
26) For as the Father hath life in himself; so hath he given to the Son to have life in himself;

30) Marvel not at this: for the hour is coming, in the which **all that are in the graves shall hear his voice,**

31) ***And shall come forth; they that have done good, unto the resurrection of life; and they that have done evil, unto the resurrection of damnation.***

Now, John 6, 10,11, and 17 put forth a similar message. And Acts 2 says:
42) And they continued steadfastly in the apostles' doctrine and fellowship, and in breaking of bread, and in prayers.

48) And fear came upon every soul: and many wonders and signs were done by the apostles.

49) And **all that believed were together, and had all things common;**

50) And sold their possessions and goods, **and parted them to all men, as every man had need.**

51) And they, continuing daily with one accord in the temple, and breaking bread from house to house, did eat their meat with gladness and singleness of heart,

52) Praising God, and having favour with all the people. And the Lord added to the church daily such as should be saved.

Acts 4 says:
30) By stretching forth thine hand to heal; and that signs and wonders may be done by the name of thy holy child Jesus.

32) And when they had prayed, the place was shaken where they

And hath made of one blood all nations of men for to dwell on all the face of the earth, and hath determined the times before appointed, and the bounds of their habitation;

28) For **in him we live, and move, and have our being;** as certain also of your own poets have said, For we are also his off- spring.

29) Forasmuch then as **we are the offspring of God,** we ought not to think that the Godhead is like unto gold, or silver, or stone, graven by art and man's device.

30) And the times of this ignorance God winked at; but now commandeth all men

And Acts 26:8 says: Why should it be thought a thing incredible with you, that God should raise the dead?

Revelation 20 says:
1) And I saw an angel come down from heaven, having the key of the bottomless pit and a great chain in his hand.

2) And he laid hold on the dragon, that old serpent, which is the Devil, and Satan, and **bound him a thousand years,**

3) And cast him into the bottomless pit, and shut him up, and set a seal upon him, that he should deceive the nations no more, till the thousand years should be fulfilled: and after that he must be loosed a little season.

4) **And I saw thrones, and they sat upon them, and judgment was given unto them: and I saw the souls of them that were beheaded for the witness of Jesus, and for the word of God, and which had not worshipped the beast, neither his image, neither had received his mark upon their foreheads, or in their hands; and they lived and reigned with Christ a thousand years.**

5) **But the rest of the dead lived not again until the thousand years were finished.** ***This is the first resurrection.***

6) **Blessed and holy is he that hath part in the first resurrection: on such the second death hath no power, but they shall be priests of God and of Christ, and shall reign with him a thousand years.**

19 IT'S NICE COMING HOME TO YOU

I smile, and hug and kiss you,
Say how great it is to see you.

I say, "I love you, Sweetheart!"
It's so good to see you!

How was your day?
Wow! You look gorgeous!
You get more beautiful every day!

You know what, Nata?
I am so lucky to have you, Honey.

I love you,
Appreciate you more each day.
And love to hear you say,
"I love you."

Let us build wisely on this love,
And make this home our very own
Castle Of Love.

20 TRYING TO COMMUNICATE WITH GOD IS HARD

OK, folks, I'm with you on this,
It's not easy to communicate with God!

Sometimes, back in the day,
I had a good thing going,
For a while.

My physical and breathing exercises
Were fantastically productive.

But I didn't know enough
To know how to use
My productivity.

I had fantastic visions, dreams.
Saw fantastic things!
WOW! Those were the days.

But, I had to work days,
And nights, or evenings.

I did not know,
So much of what I saw was "real."
I didn't understand a lot.

But, in the quiet, in the still,
There was often a kind of interaction going on.

One time, in about 1995,
I was called, three times,
Just like Samuel.

And I want to tell you something
Real important! See?

"God" is in each of us,
And we in Him.

That's how we obtain life,
I mean consciousness, awareness.

Now, I want to tell you something else, something a little strange:
Each of us represent God,
But some represent the higher forms of God,
Like justice, balance, love, mercy, faith, hope,
Benevolence,
You see?
For everything is in Him, you see that?

So, once in a while, I heard or experienced
The small, still voice.

My ten-year old son once said to me,
"We are God," meaning each of us is "God."

And that is close,
But you have to define what you're talking about.
Yes, each of us represent our own little portion of God.
But, on what level do we represent God?

Sometimes, we forget that God is death, and life,
Reaction and action, effect and cause,
Justice, that overturns injustice,
And might be harsh!
The God Force acts in many different ways:
Sometimes, it is a riddle,
Sometimes, it repeats itself three times,
Sometimes, it just appears, and smiles;
Sometimes, it's communicating important info, in our dreams,
Sometimes, it prevents you from catching the flight that crashes,
Sometimes, it warns you about a friend,

or lover, or enemy.
Sometimes, it gives you insight, or the answer to a problem.
Sometimes, He gives you bliss and joy.
Sometimes, they (or He) will answer you directly, as on 8/4/1999,
And again, on 5/2/2000, and at other times.

But it's not easy.
If it was, I'd have a lot of answers for you,
And information too.

Once in about 2002, I thought I was on a roll,
Thought I had figured out how to easily do
The Meditation Thing of 8/4/99, 5/2/00, and other times.
But, once there was too much light, to see the answer,
And sometimes too much noise, to hear;
So, take that!

Now, do unproductive times indicate that
It's not time for us to get *that* answer?
Or, does it mean we have not earned an answer yet?
Or, is there another reason?

See, in a way, we are god, with the small "g,"
For we exist in Him, getting our "god" status, force, abilities,
Through the flow of forces from Him, and them,
Higher consciousness, insight, see?

And being a part of that Collective,
Are we not party to making weather,
Hurricanes, tornadoes, and sunny days?
Creating, and destroying, justly?

Useful communication with God, (for me),
Requires ABSOLUTE integrity, in spiritual matters,

An open mind, a search for TRUTH, and facts,
Wherever the facts may lead.

It requires study, looking at history,
Seeing if what we "see" in visions, dreams, has any validity.
Does it conform to the physical world reality?

For example, I have known
About the 7th and 8th World Powers (Empires), Since 1979,
And I have watched the 8th Empire form, Beginning in about 1991, with the First Gulf War,
For, the 8th Empire is USA, UK, Canada, Australia, The European Union, NATO.

And note, the reason we want ABSOLUTE integrity, in spiritual matters,
Is because the universe is cause/effect, action/reaction, And if we put untruth, or lies, falsehoods, into the mix, How could we ever trust what we then see, or hear; you understand?
For, we will reap what we have sowed.

And is that small, still voice just us, Our Higher Self,
Telling us what we have earned a right to know?
Well, my son has a point!
The bottom line is,
That, for some, it's not even easy to realize God exists,

And even for me, a yogi, and religious student,
It's not easy to communicate with God,
And understand,
Especially, if you want an answer.

21 I KEEP COMING BACK TO THIS TASK

Trying to explain the best I can
About this force called God.

And it's not easy to get your mind around this awesome concept.

OK. Try this:
"God" is a mental construct
We create to try and understand God.

See, mind is a real place, Higher than matter,
Controlling what's below (it), Impacting things above.

The ancients constructed
God and Heaven,
With the help of God.

And we understand certain things about our universe.
About respective roles of men and women, how I should love you,
Family relations, kinship ties, community.
Said everything has its proper place and time.

We all taught reincarnation,
Love, and truth, and justice, compassion, and mercy,
The same as we received.

Said Evil Doers attract evil,
They lie and cheat and steal and kill,
And you'll know who they are.

Now, what we have to do
Is evolve much further, and try much harder,
And come back to this task.

22 BREAKFAST IN BED IS LOVELY WITH YOU

I love having breakfast in bed with you.
I love to see you, fresh and rested.
I love to see you purr, yawn, like a kitten.

I love to see you, sexy, in your robe,
And watch your beautiful morning smile,
And see the sun light in your face,

And watch you eat, slowly, deliberately,
And dutifully drink your juice and coffee.

I love to see you finish,
Happy,
Shower,

Rested, strengthened,
And thankful for a wonderful breakfast,
And ready for morning love.

23 ABOUT THE AUTHOR, AND OTHER BOOKS

Youssef Khalim obtained Unity in yoga on about 7/20/80. He says, "We will recombine into one faith, Judaism, Christianity, and Islam." He has been able to "see" and experience some amazing information about USA presidents Jefferson, Lincoln, and Obama; and also Prophets Moses, Muhammad, and Solomon - in visions, lucid dreams, and in meditation. Khalim makes reincarnation (resurrection) central again in our western religions. He resides in the Chicagoland area. And he is the father of Tonya, Runako, and Noah. See his books on the following websites: http://amazon.com, http://lulu.com, and http://sunracommunications.com

OTHER BOOKS

Youssef Khalim's books include *People Of The Future/Day; You Are Too Beautiful; I Love You Back; You Look So Good; The Resurrection Of Noah; Healing Begins With The Mind; Jubilee Worldwide; Lara, Forever; Tanisha Love; Galina, All About Love; Ekaterina, Hot and Lovely; Natalia, With Love; Svetlana, Angel Of Love; I Call My Sugar, Candie*; *Love of My Life;* and *The Second Coming!*

www.ingramcontent.com/pod-product-compliance
Lightning Source LLC
LaVergne TN
LVHW052301100826
845147LV00001B/116

* 9 7 8 0 9 7 8 7 8 1 0 6 4 *